Est. 2020

The Poetry Book III

By
Ramsey Wake

Copyrighted 2020, 2021 by Trevor Waechter

All rights reserved

Printed in the U-S of A (raleigh to be specific)

For more information concerning permissions to reproduce selections from this book email ramseywake@gmail.com

Manufactured by the manufacturer

Produced by a producer

Book designed by a designer

ISBN: 978-1-71614-931-3

Content ID: 5789187298739870000

Social Security: just kidding

"Psst let's do some poetry"
"No it's business time"
"But poetry book..no?"
"We must protect the business"
"What business"

Business Address: hmm.. he's got a point

Business Contacting and Social Media Handles: yeah, much better at poetry than this stuff

"Let's just do poetry stuff"
"Alright... whatever"

The Line-Up

Catastrophe in 2020

More Wilder

Truly Broken

Misinterpreted 70s Songs

100 Thoughts

Holidays

Geometric

Effusion

Pile of Rejects

again we emerge
ready to experience and adventure
to venture through heart, mind, and soul
in search of higher meaning and better breathing
a new opportunity
let's see if it's worth seizing

...

because we all know
the best things
come in threes

Catastrophe in 2020

humanity in 2020

we're living in a time that's frankly quite embar-
rassing
a time we've spent far too long bickering
an argument over fact
isn't time well spent.
no longer can we tolerate not seeing eye to eye
there are those with eyes and those ocularly
broken
you see the species we've hunted then desert-
ed
and when things reach levels of endangerment
there is no last ditch effort.
or if there is,
we reach out while still sitting down
humanity has reached a new peak
to coin it in phrase "mental obesity"
we break hearts freely
to crush is more satisfactory

and can be done within the reach of complacency.
embarrassing.
we freely watch some of the greatest species go extinct
we even burn our own boat and sit idly by as it sinks
we can not stand up for each other.
to those who call themselves lucky
for being birthed to a family with money
take a look around for me,
use your good circumstance practically
if you're born to a family whose name has glory
why can't you see that ?
if it's a life of selfish living,
with a large donation today
your name would be written in history
as a hero who saved planetary catastrophe.
and if you dare to say you live a life of humility,
how humiliating to watch human life across the planet
live lives that are suffered and challenged
watch species so damaged.
it's no longer the circle of life

when a piece of the wheel has so much more
weight it could carry,
for we are humanity
and it's time to prove
we have worth

clean the air

what is immortality
truly ?
could it not be practical in meaning ?
this very day
you could give away slips of green paper
in exchange for life
and in caution,
we refuse.
perhaps it's more than just selfish
perhaps there's trust issues
but to see the fire raging,
to feel the effects of the climate changing
to breathe air that's breaking
don't be mistaken,
if your home was on fire you'd be more than
uneasy.
i am angry
i am sick and tired
of watching the powerful act sleepy,
the middle class blaming,
and the poor now burning.
diminish your social que

destroy your financial restriction
and just give,
give ridiculously
give responsibly
give freely
however it must be done,
there's no time left to ignore
it's the time to ignite.
for fires need to sweep nations no longer physical
but internal
too many billions of people are cold and budgetarily selfish,
the reality being that if one billion people gave a one time donation of three dollars
peace would be restored,
our planet would thrive
in turn we would survive
feel cleaner and better.
yet many who just read that statistic scoffed,
we know to even attract one hundred people to do anything
feels impossible,
a million a joke

and a billion provides signs of insanity.
though that shouldn't stop you from doing your part
we live in a parking lot surrounded by speed bumps
but do not stop,
you drive over and you drive past
if you hit a speed bump while driving fast
you'll reach the air.
at last
you become the hero we need
the hero the planet seeks,
and maybe the speed bump will now take notice
maybe the speed bump will move an inch
it's no longer time for hopes and prayer
we fed this disaster.
now we must clean the air

the people of zero

are we truly the world's dominant species,
if we call ourselves the smartest
yet fail to see the obvious changes ?
our characteristics are resemblant
to that of an idiot,
when we didn't study the sciences in college
and ignore the ones who did
who say we are in imminent danger.
we stand on the edge of a decaying cliff
as geologists tell us it is in fact decaying,
we say we refuse to be swayed
as if fact has suddenly become an argument.
we sit in our cozy two stories
we sit in our neighborhoods with happy trees
and green in the woods,
we listen to the tv tell us about the extinction of
another species
and it doesn't change our mood.
but it changes our ecosystem
suddenly sharks cannot hunt
and many predators go unchecked
whales breath their dying breaths

fish are overcome by pests
the coral is bleached to death.
now our oceans are empty
and our diets have to change
our lifestyles now rearranged
for every bit of news we watch
and don't act,
our good conscience laxed
decay reacts,
fissioning into bitter and angry people
crafting killers.
these are 'the people of zero'
those who have given nothing
those who will give no more
their net contribution to the world
entirely self focused.
the people of zero
much like the locust

for your information

for your information,
bandages for the beaten and broken
coat less than a netflix subscription.
for your information,
every ticket sold to a train station
rather than car transportation
saves hundreds of trees from certain annihilation.
for your information,
one hundred million animals killed each year
from the material that will never disappear.
and we grow in fear
with the thought of a foreign process
to contain our goods.
we fear we will miss the plastic past
"please oh please i need the material that will always last"
see the animal,
live in it's eyes
for the extent of its existence
peaceful and consistent
focused on freeness

suddenly entangled in an inescapable mess.
the manta ray no longer able to spread its wings,
the upside down shark never again will breathe,
and the young baby turtle who's guillotined
by your friends at plastic machinery llc.
do our neighbors
who we share this earth with have any meaning ?
is there any point to our reckless killing ?
to our abandonment of the creatures we swore to look after ?
and the planet we thought we could protect ?
though we forgot,
or worse
we looked away
we let the planet decay
all that's left is flames
but it can be saved from permanent destruction.
for your information,
you may have to cancel that one subscription
to give a bandage and a prescription
before we face eviction.

don't underestimate the shift

it's easy to forget by the fourth or fifth echo and
vibration
that it had a point of origination,
that could be you
it could be me.
when mouths are opened
ears are listening
it's a fallacy of human operations,
for no matter how idiotic the opinion
our brain still processes the information.
and it seems that comments of extremity
often lands longest in the brain's memory.
no this isn't a call to say the outlandish
unless of course
you feel the outlandish needs to be said,
this is a call to rid yourself
of the falsified informations
and ditch the politics
and the politicians.
it's time to send echoes
through the caves of the brain
like a songbird's melody
we must be in harmony,

and stand as one.
the hours have gone by fast
progress still stands still,
it's time to shout with
every last piece of will
that we believe
in the forest's home
that we claim
the oceans as our own
and will no longer stand by
the fast and convenient.
we will respect the borders
of our nations,
contain our wastes,
and find healthier foods to taste.
no more processing
no more forest killings
we deserve better living.
do not my friends,
underestimate the shift.
here's our chance to be humanity's earthquake,
as we sift through walls
squeak through gaps
and illuminate against the smoke clouds.

we will not be silenced
we won't kneel to our establishment
we join in hands,
in voice
echo with great volume,
noise
they will know our names.
they will find we never change.
and in our dying hours
we will come with rage.
we will not break

outro - nearly extinct - the wild home

we are all in a big boat,
a beautiful boat
a boat which we steer.
we are captains and pioneers responsible for the care of her
because if we don't,
we lose control
and without control,
without love and care
our boat will begin to rot
it may damage and break in a few spots
and the tools to fix damages are available
but they aren't cheap.
and they aren't something you can fix on the side
they require full attention on the problem at hand,
but now comes the truth
there's a hole
a big fucking hole
a glory spout
and with it

our boat begins to sink.
naturally or, logically
all hands would be on deck
to make sure this hole is repaired
because it's not like life will just continue on,
unless we start living life underwater
no signs point to us being ready for that just yet.
who would want to anyway
we'd lose out on so much
all the beauty that our boat offers.
yet
we don't jump to action
our captains sit around and play their games
they dance the tango
hell they dump buckets of water into the hole
mocking it's very existence,
experts on boats and this boat's structural stability
say we have a very serious problem
and they have solutions
but the captains say they're wrong
the captains say even if it was an issue
'there's no way it could be serious'

certainly not worth throwing a dollar at.
experts in sinking ships say
this is certainly a candidate
but the captains decline their statements,
it's all just fake news anyways right ?
and tear down some more rainforest
we can squeeze more people in there
let's have a festival here
and a fuck fest near
oh no,
we don't need to protect anywhere
who cares about elephants
we don't need turtles
when was the last time anyone
asked for snow ?
and that
is not
a hole.
"we
are not
sinking."
call us hippies for noticing the planets change,
call us new age for listening to scientists,

call us the generation who doesn't get shit done,
while you sit idly by
not getting shit done.
have you ever considered cutting your plastic intake ?
carpooling to cut emissions ?
have you ever volunteered for anything ?
history will remember this decade,
and the people who said 'we couldn't'
'we wouldn't'
'we didn't.'
but what if instead
they remembered us as the generation that changed
the generation that saw
what previous generations missed
the generation that plugged the hole
the generation that kept the boat floating
that's the generation id be proud to be apart of
a world that i'd be happy to live in
regardless of our employment status,
our educational dropout percentages,
a stat that says we did our part.

we set aside differences
and made a difference
and a message that comes with the price of sacrifice
that we all made to save,
'love truly does conquer.'
if not for each other
than a love to be alive.
a love to survive,
a love of something that lives,
and a will,
to not sit by
and watch the living and spinning beauty
that some call earth
to be choked and burnt down.
instead to see her strive
to be her hero in this dying hour
and look after the blue and green place
that we call home.
a wild home.

fusion pt.1 (a wild processing of catastrophe)

clearly

closing your eyes is a quick and sudden revelation:
this world has so much more to offer than just sight.
a strong redwood scent,
a gentle breeze that dances through hair gracefully,
the sound of ocean waves rolling onto beaches in crashes.
just close your eyes
forget everything that involves you
forget everything you've ever made for yourself
and just be there in that moment,
feeling
so many times we become caught up in the struggle of perception,
how we look to others

how others look to us,
and we forget that wherever you are
you are apart of that place.
in that moment
listen to the birds chatter
hear the people's laughter,
but drown out those that are shouting at each other.
if you must open your eyes, clean them first
look for the beauty that's in front of us so vastly
not the pretty women or men
not the pretty car or house
not the shop nor restaurant
look into the cracks in the sidewalk if you must,
but there you must find
that soil.
that earth is where the true beauty is
once you start looking at it
and looking for it
your vision will become so clear.
the clarity of this planet will become so much more meaningful
true beauty isn't obtainable by the things we build with machines.

true beauty is maui in the summer
washington in the winter
and california in every season,
see those dancing trees
feel that mountain breeze
while you gaze on mountain peaks
standing on a mountain peak
while you dream of conquering every mountain
you've ever seen.
sorrow will slowly flee
for you've become a visionary,
for earth's most pure conquest
it's beautiful soil.
let the joy of seeing clearly
be all that you seek
and may feeling wild
finally restore your soul
and become more.

More Wilder

as we are pushed to the edge of extinction
we find ourselves driving all night long.
and by dawn
we become innovatively entertained
by great schemes and truly crazy things,
now enriched we again see clearly.
we must choose love
and choose it intentionally
we must not focus our spotlight on disaster
and instead draw focus towards
those who lay dormant,
waiting for the purpose that we can show.
we loved on a wisp and received vision
and with that,
our mission became simple;
help bees
plant trees
and save the seas.

driving by dawn

driving by dawn
wildly in love.
deeply rooted you realize
this isn't enough.
rows of houses
they look the same.
it starts to feel like
no one knows my name.
but someone sings it somewhere
somewhere away from here,
where the altitude is higher
where my eyes see things more clear.
ocean breeze seized my fragile soul
i break and restore with each inhale.
with every wave my mental haze washes away
i'm reminded that my roots drift in soft sand
and are wrapped into the cliffside rock.
how long i stare into the ocean's vastness
and wonder if someone sits on the other coast
and looks for me
as i look for them.

great schemes and crazy things

great schemes and crazy things
stupid dreams and unbelievable deeds,
the world is ready.
no.
the world is desperate.
when it's time to change the world
and you feel it inside
you must change it.
you are the loaded revolver
ready to fire
you are the active human evolver
it's when you trade in your suburban home
for a life of travel
that you're onto something.
it's when you give up on waste
and go out of your way
to not live the same,
because without trash
you're onto something.
saving an animal that needs saving
researching something that needs changing

speaking out when you only want to hold it in, that's when
you're onto something.

innovatively entertained

where once we appreciated stretched out beauty,
like thousand page books
now there's six second videos.
where once we saw
visually stunning things that leave us elsewhere
now we have littered junk on social media,
just one generation away from forgetting the encyclopedia.
i wonder
where did it all go so wrong ?
but i'm not mad
forgive me for my tone.
and forgive my rabbit trails
they tend to tail
more directions
than my original poetic intentions.
what is truly sad is the perpetual hostility to be different.
not knowing memes seems to be something
equal in crime to head-butting
punching

and good ol' fashioned people hunting.
i understand
in a day and age where technology is proclaimed
'king of communication'
so forth sparks the need for new language.
and there's no better place to hide and think than behind a screen.
where did we all go so wrong ?
conversation has evolved bitterly
face to face
eye to eye
it's become so uncomfortable.
the lack of pixels in someone's profile is no longer suitable
so instead we talk robotic,
voice to voice
faces down like we're bobbing for apples
fingers flying like goldfish in a shaking bottle.
truthfully
we're bobbing for pictures with funny captions
dreaming that their contents will bridge enough gaps
that bond will be created.

a bond to bondage
would you believe me if i told you
i met people that looked up what someone
looked like
when they were looking right at them ?
i've seen it
you may have too,
where did we take this so far ?
i am ridiculed for avoiding the outside world,
my world so very silent
as i cower deep inside my shell
deeply disturbed by recent times.
for when people speak
the words feel very weak
or aggressively attacking,
their relation to the understanding
of the ways in which i interact with the world
it's severely lacking.
being different is a dangerous game
because people will give you exactly what you
want
if the goal is to avoid timid interaction
the world will give you an answer:
ostracization.

cast out status.
banded together with those they've bonded with
socialites make sure you know exactly how odd you are
and somehow we have to take those punches.
i question why sometimes.
why must we need to be true to ourselves?
if the rest of the world would rather you lie.
perhaps because being different isn't something that's meant to be shared with the surplus population
just one or two
who think the same way you do.
there will only be the few,
is that enough for you ?
i'm not speaking on the ones
you call them your 'crew'
you take pictures to send to dudes
and make others jealous in order to increase your mood.
the few are entirely different.
these are the true few,
who listen
understand your vision

come to their own decisions,
follow in the footsteps of your mission
and together you form fission.
when you fall down, they help sing a new song
and help you find a place to belong
because the wild ride
doesn't last long.
so swallow their derogatory demands
let them monologue on,
listen to them describe what we are supposed
to look like
and in response to how many fucks we should
give,
there's just one answer
none.
look like you
talk like you
the rest will follow suit.

i chose love

i chose love
to negate hate,
leaving pain
as my only fate.
for love is a promise
i kept dear,
a vow to appreciate
and not degrade
fight
instead of forget.
be there then,
in that moment
in that place,
search for what's good
instead of the various reasons of it being bad.
i'm not saying
i'll become more positive
i'm not saying
i'll accept more people into my life
i'm not even saying
that i'll smile when i'm smiled at.
what i mean is when i'm thrown under the bus

when i'm mocked and tormented
when i'm gossiped about
when i'm cornered and removed from my comfort zone
i will remain calm.
i will refuse to spit on graves
i will refuse to speak out against
i will not fight back unless it's absolutely necessary.
i'm tired of accusing this world of it's beastiality
it's chaotic violence
and the lack of good spirits,
while i sit
and grumble
and fight.
i know my soul is belligerent
but i have to teach myself
how to break free of that restless aggression,
there is something to be said about
a soul disturbance as a casualty of not being
where you need to be,
and in acknowledging that
you are lost into a multiverse of frustration

as you try to decipher why you stay in places
that only bring great pain.
but life puts you in pens
not palaces,
it's your job to end up
where you intend on going.
if your ship is landlocked
and you're left marooned on an island,
choose love.
the effort of not fighting against a scenario you
cannot change
could free you to new peace you didn't know
you could find,
our souls are fragile in pursuit of happiness
crazy schemes and idiotic dreams
and love.
a splash of wild heart
is all you need

spotlight focus

our heavy set eyes
they are set heavily on the future.
humanity fears surprises,
and rightfully so.
those practical pranks played by people
with proprietary power often end without a punchline.
or rather they end with a group of people standing in a line
to be punched with knuckles firmly intertwined.
our spotlight focus so set on those who change our future
we forget our own nature.
we forget that being human means being stubborn,
being emotionally outspoken,
being different from others in our species.
we forget that being human means owning the right to change what you feel needs to be.
and not to say everything should be changed or needs to be,
but to say that when the time comes

and your stomach churns in disapproval
and you feel kindling set in your soul
you don't analyze any further.
you don't dissect or depict
you resist rest and you detest against the rest
the change you fight for becomes a test
are you willing to let it go and fail ?
or raise yourself above,
and become the best.
and see that change be made in your lifetime
so that the next member of your bloodline can make another change
instead of changing the change that you should've changed.
it would be preposterous to ask someone to drop what they've held for longer than they've known how to hold
to drop something they've saved for when they're old
but to be wild is something that can't be sold
to be wild
is to be bold

disaster

people come,
go.
people enter,
exit.
we walk into tunnels,
blinded.
we walk out into what's new,
stronger.
the engine runs until it doesn't,
broken.
we surround ourselves with mechanics,
fixed.
we live,
opportunity.
we die,
missed.
for every action,
there is an inopportune moment
waiting to happen.
disasters are chances to fall apart uncontrol-
lably,
but did you realize

these are chances to rewrite your story ?
you say you hate who you are
but there's the chance for new identity
always.
you just have to work for it
it's as easy as putting your trash on the doorstep
it's as easy as saying goodbye to everything you've kept.
we are cars in a car lot
over time we depreciate,
our knots do not stay tot
for we are made of rope
and the rope does rot.
it's as simple as you live
if you don't get shot.
we feel destructive,
change.
we go back to our old ways,
shame.
we wish and pray to go a new way,
procrastinate.
debate.
stalemate.

so we stay destructive
for fear of disaster,
irony.
i'm not saying let go of the wheel
but when you lose your wheels
don't sit and sulk,
don't fear.
you're now more free than most of us in that moment
finally
wild and free.
now when i lose everything
i sit back smiling
i can become anything i want
my slate is clean.
we hit disaster,
laugh.
we feel terror,
fight back.
we are free,
wild.

loving on a wisp

if given the chance to love any one person of my choosing
i would pick someone i've never met.
and why that would be
i'm still trying to decide.
maybe because everyone i've met walks with too much pride,
maybe i just haven't found anyone who's capable of taking me out of myself,
and maybe that's more fantasy
than possibility.
but i need it to be true
if i intend on loving again
i need someone who doesn't necessarily understand me now,
but studies
as i learn to understand them as well.
someone who's not fearful of danger
if it's in pursuit of something greater,
than the damage it takes to get there.
but it's also possible that i choose the unknown option

for the beauty of exploration,
a new journey to a place
that isn't of this planet or dimension,
rather into a soul, mind, and heart.
and though so often disappointed by the casual approach
and the constant blockades built by peers to prevent prying and peering eyes,
in this dream scenario where love is the only option
we could freely break down barriers
we could peak into the mind
find love in the areas hidden from the bright city lights.
we all have mental forests with trails,
that if followed long enough
end somewhere brilliant.
i am a trail runner
and to explore every trail i can,
it is my act of love.
for the further i go,
the more i can map.
and the more i understand,
the more i have to enjoy

and love.
we all filter our output for fear of being misun-
derstood, outcasted, or uninteresting
but being weird shouldn't mean being alone
it just means you belong with better people.
the crazy crowd that knows this world should be
danced on
not walked
not flown through
or off of.
if only there was a wild group like this,
if only we all danced,
if we did
we could all find each other a bit easier.
but until then we continue to wish for crazy
dreams of love
and continue to say maybe,
and what if,
as we dance
with ourselves
alone.

dormant

i am dormant.
hibernating.
like a bear, i am vicious
dangerous when my soul is awakened.
don't startle me,
i am startled by the obvious attacks directed my way.
down here in this cage,
i am dormant.
i am the hibernating bear dangerously
vicious by souls awakened.
with sole intention
of obvious attacks that are directed in my direction.
they lock me in cages,
i am dormant.
but even in this state,
do not mistake,
i am lethal.
belligerence and rage are two things
one in the same
but can be channeled

in deathly one-two combinations
that will not only break cages
but break faces.
no tranquilizer touches me when i lose control,
that's why I keep my lid sealed tight
i stay put
i remain dormant.
my lethal state
filled with deathly combinations
so complicated,
like a maze with multiple exits
one exit's to the belligerent
the other to rage,
and both will break a face.
but i allow the tranquility to defeat me,
because some fights are better lost
so i can keep control.
the only way to keep from spilling fluids
is to keep the lid sealed tight,
dormant.
but allowing for passive channeling and outlets
to draw power productively,
placing it into areas
not so destructive,

and much more legal,
poetic.
less lethal.
though words on pages
leads to deeper mental cages,
complicated, unprocessed, and blended emotions,
mental sanity escaping deeper into the void.
what am i really ?
a bear ?
i doubt it.
a person ?
less likely.
troubled ?
surely.
but troubled is not a name.
am i rage,
am i belligerence,
am i nothing but a wrecking ball
that swings only at myself
destroying what i try and build ?
only on the weekends.
what i truly am,
i have been saying this whole time.

i am dormant.
and if i am half of what i think i am,
i fear what will come
when i awake.

jumpstart

with so much deceit
i forget what you truly are.
why do you hide your face in plain sight ?
you ask for a platform
and an ear to listen
but when it's presented,
you cower.
fucking coward.
you have a blend
never before seen
you are a true one of one
why hide ?
there's not much to offer outside of that fate
anyways,
yes they'll call you strange,
foreign,
dangerous,
and they're right.
you are exactly those things
is that so wrong ?
they'd tell you yes.
but they fear what they don't understand,

and that's exactly what you keep forgetting,
that's when you keep giving up
you see their fear
and you believe
you never made to be an antagonist.
we don't get to pick whether we are villains or heroes
that 's the job of the public.
what matters is that their fear
is an acceptance that your role is more important
than the average mind
comprehends.
that means you have a platform,
say something,
that means anything
or
say anything,
and have it mean something.
how it's accepted
that's out of our hands.
you are a messenger of feeling
and they may shoot you for spreading the word,
but that's foreign policy.

entering new territory and displaying technology,
or in this case ideology,
about how you feel
things could be improved.
to theorize and spread dreams,
asking to be proven wrong
these are aggressive tactics indeed.
and shouldn't be expected to be received
with open arms.
though i acknowledge that is the wish
maybe one day,
with a bit of luck,
you'll meet a him or her
and they will fall in love with your brilliance
understand every sentence as it exits your mind.
but reality says
it's not the likeliest path.
and for that.
you must prepare.
prepare for that worst case
where everyone hates what you say.
they lead you to a world where

you can see every corner at the same time.
a world where you wear jackets
that keeps you from scratching out your eye-
balls.
or they exile you
to the coldest island.
that's their choice,
hate them for it.
they will still act on it,
prepare for the fight along the way.
even if sentenced to dig your way to hell
along the way someone will remember what
you've said
while you stood,
and maybe they will process it.
come to a conclusion;
you weren't evil
you weren't harmful
you just thought the natural world should be
more appreciated.
you found new ways to love it,
you found new ways to love others,
maybe that one individual

though not daring enough to share with the
lethal public,
but maybe even for just him or her,
they will apply some of your thoughts
into their life subconsciously.
and that's enough.
one will understand you
even in the slightest,
that's what all this is about.
someone or some people,
who understand the chaos
without knowing you at all.
coherence is an issue here
but that's just it,
you weren't even supposed to read this.
consider it a jumpstart in a race
you weren't trying to win.

the pacific

i feel cold far from home
one would guess it's a result of the colder climate
and physically,
they have a point.
but weather cannot touch a soul
or can it,
because salty air and misty breezes
move me to different places,
cool refreshing air that tastes clean to the touch
it cleanses my dirtied soul
and lights fires that keep me at perfect temperature.
but now i just feel cold
the humid stick of uncomfortably sweaty stickiness clogging my exit points,
the foggy brain feeling of finding yourself fighting for relief.
this place is ruthless and offers no escape,
no ocean to dunk your head in
no ocean within a hundred miles is a crime and a sin,

i'm sure to others the ocean is nothing more
than a body of water.
but to me it is home
and it will always be my first wife
my first love.
it's become my everything,
her cliff sides are the rocks i build upon
her depth is my explanation for deep exploration.
i feel cold without her
i yearn for her waves
i pray for her surf
i miss her soundscape,
and the way she dances to her own beat
a truly free specimen.
she has that eye
same as a puppy on their first walk,
the look of a bear in the wild
or of a calm rabbit
it's the eye of freedom,
true freedom.
to be free of worry
with no "i wish i could've" from the past
with no "i wish i will" in the future

just moments,
by moments
by moments.
just smiles
by surfs
by grandeur
look no further,
it doesn't get better.
the greatest most wild body
the pacific

permanence

something truly powerful is something that has
no ending,
something we will never be able to look back
on,
it will either
never be written into history
or will be written in every book.
it doesn't matter how many numbers you put up
against it
or how much money you throw it's way
it will continue all the same,
it's why we rage at politicians
and their wishy-wash decision making.
it's why we don't buy the house
why we do buy the plane ticket
that takes us to the places we remember
forever.
sometimes the most permanent things
are the memories that only last a few moments,
imagine just minutes of one day
which you'll have thousands more in the future,
and have had thousands in the past.

having such significance
that it stays embedded with you
for the rest of your life.
we all have these minutes,
that childhood memory
horrible breakup story
heroic athletic accomplishment
that first performance
it's different for all of us.
but these minutes will become our stories
they will try to define who you are,
nobody will care where you were before these minutes
or where you went after.
like summiting a mountain
the trek to the top,
perhaps more monumental than the actual
moment of reaching that peak,
but nobody looks at the pictures of the trek up.
they want to see how high you reached
and that moment,
that picture,
becomes a piece of your permanence.
the lasting memories of who you were

a beautiful thought,
but also terrifying
historical murderers only remembered for their crimes
failed politicians and scientists
all remembered as failures
not as people who pushed progression.
that is where permanence will soil what you've built
because once you've been placed into the box of crazy and dangerous,
there is rarely an escape.
not to justify crime
but to say
where did forgiveness and love run so dry ?
we used to stand by each other's side
and defend each other until it wasn't possible.
if there is a place we go after death
won't that too be permanent ?
wherever we go
i am starting to understand permanence,
not as a measurement of time
or as a point of afterlife
but as a way to live.

love can't be mistaken
caring for others will only build permanence
here on earth,
and wherever after,
in both cases
love must be appreciated on some level.
and i'd rather have my permanence here be known
as the one
who showed love to the loveless
cared for the homeless
and lived a truly wild life.
this isn't a promise for now,
this is a permanent tie i'm tying
a guarantee that i will continue to improve
until i have built my permanence here.
and on the chance there's something after,
i will know i only did my best
here

fusion pt.2 (Wildly Broken)

safe place

part of me knows
this is a joke
albeit sad and twisted,
but in a laughable way.
like a joke that makes you cringe inside
but you look back and you laugh,
maybe because it's not so serious.
connections are hard to come by
and even the planes that land
take off
on a later day
and the only way we can cope with the turn
over
is by doing it often,
repeat disaster until it becomes desensitized.
the true joke is how i looked down on the shop-
pers
the door to door salesmen and women

and now a piece of me gets it.
because by the millionth time you fall face first
into the mud
you wear it for a while,
you pretend that it's war paint
and you're a soldier at war
you roll around a bit because
why the fuck not ?
and eventually you've fallen so much
you're prepared.
the pain doesn't follow,
instead comes humor
a part of me now understands
this built in defense system
the rest of me knows
it'll never be something that would actually
work.
love by definition is intense
and intensity,
though can be faked to the eye,
cannot be acted.
the action itself requires respect for the one you
are doing the action to or for
and to deliver the action one million times,

would exhaust the body to a point where
neurologically the brain would tell the heart to
just stop pumping,
to put an expiration on respiration,
turn thoughts to memories.
some of us will struggle to love someone
many of us will fail completely
few of us will be a great blend of lucky and
wise,
where man will meet his bride
and bride will love the guy,
the few deserve congratulations.
that's why they call for large celebrations
where the rest dream
that it'll one day be us
who finds that dear thing love.
most of us probably won't
we will marry more than once,
end up in scenarios we fight hard for
and fail
scenarios, truly not even worth swinging a
punch over.
"all you need is love" is probably true
but we as humans

who stray from what scares us
deny the probability of love needing us.
love needs no one
it prefers a chase,
like a dog that does not love the ball
until sent into motion.
so depressive then
but it doesn't have to be
and this is the point i make,
lots of us are horrible people
not on purpose
but causality of human nature points to us be-
ing slightly more fucked up
than the average creature
it's hard for us to love people when we are con-
stantly attacking.
so i raise this thought
that love, that's bound inside your body
that love, you keep giving away to the wrong
people
invest it elsewhere.
invest into art
or artistically crafted music
or musically made sculptures

or photographing the mountain to poster.
there's plenty of world to exist in, surely
but possibly more importantly
there's plenty of world to love.
and if you can't wake everyday
and drive someplace that you would call amazing
what are you doing ?
what is money in the face of love ?
does love not best all other cards in the deck ?
there are endless forests
jungles
cities to explore,
places you'll come to love.
places that may make you love yourself
a place to start over
or just start,
these places look different to all of us
and they should.
but don't wonder when you'll get to this place
or if you even can
you must.
pent up love will leak out and chemically adapt into

aggression
restlessness
emptiness.
you need to reach these places at all costs
you must get home,
and find love
in your work or home or lifestyle
preferably all three.
and never give up until you feel strongly
you are where you need to be,
a place your heart feels
wild
safe
and free

it's alright

it's been so long since
i last felt alright.
deep cuts keep me bleeding
like ripped iv bags,
everyday has become a question
of which day is the last day
that i can withstand the pain.
with no release
no freedom
torture by means of mental insanity
has me on the edge of my mental state.
readily available to cross borders
into the state over from mine
and lose any hope i had
of salvaging pieces of myself.
a recurring theme in this book is the word "alright"
it seems you have to lie for a while
before it becomes your truth,
sometimes you have to lie face down
and release every ounce of energy you have

hope that some of the demons that break your back leave.
these demons are bigger than my brain
the guilt i'd feel if i lost them
they're all i have left of what i once loved,
and i don't love too much anymore.
just the quiet.
it's alright
i'll shake it off
i'll get back into the lineup
one of these days,
one day i'll have the doctor check out my eyes properly
and buy that prescription
that fixes my lens of life.
everything's so dark
so blurry
i see fear and death walking down the street,
i see anxiety's terrible face making out with my depression.
i don't care to see them any longer,
they are not my friends
i'd rather be friendless
they are not my names

i'd rather be nameless.
the hauntings that come to me in the night
cannot hold my soul anymore
i will take back my peace of mind
and hold it tight
like it's all i have left.
and then it'll all be alright
but how ?
as if to imagine
i haven't been trying already,
these are just empty promises
until the war actually concludes.
if there's a fight
it will be on my soil
in my soul's most clear trail,
the path to the mountain
the dirt that takes me to the redwoods.
all the way home
amongst the green shrubbery
breathing ocean air that's misting
sites of wildlife living life wildly
a sun that operates
on a very specific schedule
a million stars that bring light to the sky

reinforcing me in my fight.
yes
this is where i will make my stand,
regain what i lost.
a wild heart has to fight wildly
to remain wild
and when you lose sight of that,
when the struggles become all too real,
don't fight alone
or in your suburban home.
get back to where it all starts
to the place where you most belong
then you'll see
it'll all be alright

truly broken

truly broken

what was once just feeling.
a slight disturbance to perfection
blossomed into silent whisper,
it said "love only lasts so long".
though canned foods have no best by date
eventually all things go bad,
whether it be centuries
decades
or our few years,
no promise could have prepared me less
than the promises we shared.
promises of permanence
promises of connection
and i held on so tight,
i held with both hands
until my knuckles turned white,
until my hands bled
the scars becoming irreversible,

i felt my bones scrape against the floor
as i tried to hold strong
my rib cage expanding
as my heart swelled uncontrollably.
i remember you
you were kind
had a caring spirit
and were brave.
whatever i was
i wasn't enough
i was fragmented pieces
from many assorted puzzles
all thrown into the same box together,
desperately lost and confused.
and while most of that hasn't changed,
when our expiration date passed
when all of my skin was scraped off
and my skeleton hands could no longer hold,
i learned loneliness like i never knew.
don't get me wrong
i've known how to function alone since i was young
and filled with a friendless past,
but like a man raised in poverty

eating nothing but rotten foods and garbage
who gets to taste a five star meal
it becomes entirely more difficult
to return to where you've come from.
and where i was once a friend of royalty
i am again the friend of no one
i am left with nothing to nurture
nobody to give my thoughts
nobody to share my feelings.
i pushed myself outside of my own body
so i had someone to talk to
i gave names to the animals
and listened to what i imagined they'd say
hell i even befriended the demons
that haunt my sleep.
clearly investing isn't my strong suit
to put so much stock in one place
isn't a wise practice
no matter how strong it would seem
life and the law of nature
both point to distance being more reasonable
than attraction.
the whispers change
they feel less subtle in the darker days

now that the leading voices have gone quiet
presumably moving on to better places
and greener pastures.
leaving just i
the interpreter of emotion,
and the whispers
they remind that moving on from the best
is harder than waiting for the next generation
of phone products to be released.
because this phone i'll have to build myself,
where i've been lucky before
i must now rely on my ability
to do it myself.
i must plant my own seeds
the farm i gave away
is mine to care for again.
though no matter how much work i put into it
i know no plant planted will grow to be as beautiful
as what i had before,
maybe there's something out there that can redefine beauty
for me
restore me with new meaning.

i am not yet strong enough to farm
but in the next season
my strength may return
and i just hope that once i am ready to plant again
that i do not continue to let my past break me
that i do not eat the expired food
that i let go
and i build.
and i tend to them the same way i tended to
that small plant
that i loved so dearly.

inherent darkness

is there escape from permanence ?
the harmfulness of my internal imploding
raging fits of violence
is far from marvelous,
but mental warfare points to no armistice.
the ordinance has fallen
the eminence of merciless rageful turbulence
reigning from my clenched fists
teaches why my heart feels fearfulness
in its deepest valve.
fearful of my own belligerence,
what hope do i have against the infinite ?
for even when i'm intimate i feel infamous
the indefinite timer ticks towards an imminent
power hit,
hide the innocent infant
for it's become legitimate that i might drop it
from the summit
after i fail to handle it delicate.
some people call violence magnificent
others say it is a deliberate incident
by those who are insolent,

i believe it is a coincident
for the literate who want to see something different.
what the fuck can i do
if i can't process my rage ?
the backstage misgauge of my mind's mental state
has led to an ice age,
killing off the many
leaving the rest in the cage.
in the cage we caught plague
our rage takes over
and flips to a new page,
if this is my dying fate
i hope i never find a mate
i hope i don't die in this state
i hope my death is worth the wait.
and i hope if the time comes around
i can have a new slate,
i don't hesitate or wait
i walk it clean and straight
i do not deny this fate
or take the bait.
i discover my other trait

and open a floodgate
to create
donate
and locate
my inner starting place.
hope lights the end of tunnels
even when they're inherently dark violent funnels.

big screen

we all have faces that we see everywhere
those faces you see on the big screen
but they don't match the actor or celebrity
but rather a person you love,
that's been buried in your memory.
it seems like every movie i see
you played a role,
any character's speech about how
'one should never give up on love'
'get her back'
'love all you can'
are just sparks that point to your fire.
i wish i could say that i'm actively pushing you
out of my headspace
but i can't,
i still need you there
or maybe i don't
but i certainly feel like i do.
in reality
does anybody
truly need somebody ?
i question

would i have been better off never knowing
that humanity existed
i think mowgli maybe had the best chance
at true happiness.
i'd rather die primitively
to the snake's chokehold
than feel your breath breathing through another
god damn character
on another fucking show that you know
you have no business being in.
why can't i be left alone
even when i'm alone you're there
telling me to be better than that,
ironic
that all of this space
that's gathered between us
and i need a whole lot more
or a whole lot less.
i can't keep this game up
this game is fucked
and it's tearing me apart.

misunderstood

it's nearly impossible to put into words
what it means to be so misunderstood.
there's so much to be credited for,
to others who have shunned me when i've been myself
to the rest who praise the grotesque shadow face i wear in place of my own true identity
to myself for never taking the hard road to self respect.
through my own journey of enlightenment i've learned that my truest form was never meant to be popular
so why bother ?
what's the point in worrying about fake friends who only care for an image that doesn't represent the trueness of your spirit ?
the deeper you train this character the more misunderstood you become.
learning to love yourself may not be a reality,
and i don't believe it has to be,
love is hard to come by and the chance of loving any one individual for some of us is a low

chance,
and i don't see why the rules would change for self indulgent loving,
we simply have too much love for the few who are really worth it to us
and too much love to things that can't see the love for themselves.
so misunderstood.
i am just a hand hidden behind the pen it's holding
i am just vocal chords hidden by words on pages
i am a lost human being who's trying to decide who i really want to be,
at this point i am daily fighting for that inner core presence to stay alive
yet daily i hide him underneath several layers of fake personality,
an upfront lie to those i share presence with
a statement that i'm not good enough in this environment,
but i want to be heard,
im tired of sounding stupid and hating the words that actively escape my chamber,

even though these sounds are coming from within and leaving they leave permanent burn marks as they go,
another chance to say something worth meaning,
and ending up saying nothing at all.
i want to be felt,
i want my words to touch others in a way that they think something differently
like crisp nights with a clear view of the milky way
that feeling of refresh,
something new but comfortable.
but before i can become that i must become myself,
and that means leaving these old barbaric worlds where my name has climbed ranks in pursuit of glory,
leaving them behind and not looking back on the torture i pushed myself through to gain that seniority.
i have failed many times,
and until i really feel comfortable in my skin i will probably fail again and again until i land myself

in the place i truly need to be,
with the people who truly love me
the people who i truly need.
currently misunderstood,
break free,
life is soon to be good.

the toy

out of the box
i'm not an immediate source of joy and happiness
my colors are not super silly
i look overly industrious
maybe a little boring.
you pull my string but i remain silent
too reclusive to use my voice
that's a lot of pressure to put on a new toy
one chance to say something that is equally catching and loved with enough enthusiasm to be heard over and over again.
it's much easier to say nothing
but a toy never gets to be a chooser
i'll never be a chooser and with my broken voice box
it often feels like i'll fail to be chosen
born into the shelf life.
forced to watch my peers connect
rival toys take up new lives
while i sit and wait for..
for what

i don't even know.
i may not seem the silliest on the outside
but how preposterous it is to turn away opportunities to pursuit a phantom possibility
that perfect pairs exist in this reality.
so to everyone who pulls my string
with expectation that my catchphrase will land in the lap of satisfaction
im sorry
i'm just not that kind of toy.
those who were looking for a silly and comically relieving character
care to follow me to the next aisle.
eventually my shelf life will pass
my opportunities all listed off as inopportune moments and missed chances
my silenced voice box have forced me to the nearby dump
where finally i hope to finally find my kin
searching through other people's garbage is where i've found the best toys
toys like me who aren't perfect and have no intention of pretending to be
toys who have defects but are working on them

and one day we will become the collectibles
we will be searched for through the rubble
and someone will pull my string and hear the lack of sound
and consider me priceless.
who knows
they may even fix my broken pieces.
maybe phantom possibilities are just dreams
maybe it's not so bad to wait on them for a while.

broken again

the phone rings
but i don't answer
my phone blinks
but i already know who.
though not blocked from her messages
there's a block from picking up the phone,
i am blocked to say something back.
maybe i don't have a backbone
but sneaking by on the back road
will always assure
i get back home
where i can continue to be alone.
not to say
that's truly what i want
but the bundle package that comes with people
is a world built up and torn down,
for every good moment
a bad one is stored into a vault for a later day.
i'm told there are better people out there
there are people who would rather tear them-
selves then rip through my guts
i've heard it for a decade.

waiting is a weird place
if we all wait then nothing
will ever be accomplished
but for every time i extend a hand
there's a blood-thirsty leech who seeks to eat.
whether it's intentional
or something that just happens
it doesn't truly matter,
i breed disasters.
so i look inward through my heap of emotions
an elaborate maze
that i've only just begun to map successfully,
i see many faults
enough to decay relationships
over and over
leaving me perpetually alone.
the phone rings again
it's you
and i remember how
you loved that
the world hated me
and i hated the world.
i reach for the phone
break me again

goodbye, dear rocket

you can't say goodbye to someone
who hasn't left yet,
though physically non-existent
your aura remains prominent.
a ghost that follows through the night
like how i can hear your footsteps right now
but can't look into your eyes.
nothing more painful comes to mind
than the way i felt your warmth
and now feel nothing inside,
because lava doesn't last
it burns your core and becomes rock.
you can't stop evolving,
like a rocket
you can only keep going
until you've hit the very thing
to which you were aiming.
i was just another asteroid
becoming the very thing
i was trying to help you avoid,
a hinderance,
blockades that stop you

from where you want to go.
but you are a rocket
rockets don't need help from asteroids
except in that they stay
out of the way.
i understood that,
yet wanted to help anyway
i couldn't stay away,
the fucked up law of attraction.
but as you blazed on by
your fire lit my heart alive
like i've never felt before,
like all those years floating in space
revolving around saturn's rings
was a pointless waste.
now that time spent together
feels like it was only just seconds
but that is the time
i will remember as my greatest moments.
i cherish them
i cherish you
for being my inspiration
making my life more interesting
if only for just a minute

at the capital price.
my movements interfere with your trajectory
and though just a slight tap
i am now out of orbit,
far from what i've known
and lost helplessly.
the fire inside now cold
what it melted,
never reassembled.
broken like a cold sun
permanently looking at the universe i've always known
as it gets smaller and farther away.
my inevitable question,
would i trade the life i had
a life in the world
a life that isn't too bad
not too great,
for a chance that could've changed everything
and failed,
left to a permanence
that's all too sad.
but ever so often
i feel it

the fire scorching my core
at unbelievable strength,
maybe this
is how stars are made.

august 22nd

i'm feeling more than i can bear to contemplate
this is raw and unprocessed,
mainly i just miss you.
things spiral out of control
without your patient mind around,
it kept me in place
it gave me reason
to keep a steady pace,
and to make peace
before i bring pain.
i miss studying your vastness
the many layers of your reasoning
careful contemplation
that managed to remain fun and youthful,
a voice that made my evil
feel good for a while.
eyes that broke oceans apart
eyes of natural disaster,
all that
packaged so small
in a loveable friendly size.
i lost that

i lost you
i'm not even completely sure why
but i know it hurts,
and that the chances of us speaking again
only decline with time.
which breaks my soul apart
everyday
in new ways,
and for months
i've been a hostage
trying to decide what i should do.
every new person i meet
i think of you
and it soils the new,
every new place i go i think of where we've been
and it soils again.
every meal i've consumed
stale and distasteful to my palet
i can't shake it
like drug dependence.
you were a high
that is impossible to reach again
now i'm left diseased

incapable of pushing past the past.
and the half hearted
'how long will this last ?'
but i know
i'm still gripping onto these pains
i don't wash the stains
because having a memory
is still greater
then having nothing.
i'm not prepared to move on
i feel
i have so much left to show you
and even more to learn,
though sometimes
i am forced to step back
and reminisce.
i fill with anger as i think
was it truly all that good ?
are you truly everything i make you out to be ?
at the time i was convinced that you
were the greatest thing on earth,
but then there's our final trip
those cold days in november
just a few days scattered

into a long friendship.
yet they are bright
undeniably obvious
and my mental cinema plays them often
i would love to say
it wasn't truly you.
that you felt helpless and alone
pressured to change
to fit into a new ecosystem.
but a doubt is strongly rooted in me
and within it
a theory,
that was more you
than i'd ever seen.
that before you left
you were feeling
helpless and alone
and feeling pressure to adapt to scenarios
you couldn't care for,
just to fit the old ecosystem.
that i was impeding your progress
that i kept you down while you were rising.
or even less
i was just someone

just another face
from another neighborhood.
it would feel so great to my spirit,
in a twisted way
to think,
posthumously i left an impression on you.
that maybe now that we've gone separate paths
you'd stop and think about me
in a lonely moment
and you'd regret our departing.
but a doubt is strongly rooted in me
and with it
a theory
with me clear of mind
life is much simpler.
breath comes much lighter
now you can fully buy into a new ecosystem
free of all the past
and why would you waste a moment of free
thought
on what is old and complex
than on the endless potential of the future ?
you wouldn't.
you would keep looking forward

and i know this,
yet
about a year later
all i think about is you.
cursed
and haunted
fucked all together,
love is hopeless
and people are worthless
this much i know.

outro

once again
we've processed great threat.
this section is always so hard to write
a collection of things
nobody wants to see or read,
we all wish we could be free of worry
and of the pain
for which we are all truly sorry.
nobody likes to be broken
and we've all fallen
into the darkness,
and to the few of us
who've been hit harder than the others
who know no matter how hard we try
we are broken permanently.
may the big screen no longer be a bother
and though the you
you are today may never move on
i hope one day you can sing a song
without them in mind
all day long.

because like broken engines under the car's hood
we are truly misunderstood,
but like a toy
we can be mended and repaired.
one day i'm sure someone could,
but until then
we only get broken
again and again.
as i did on august twenty-second
when i was forced to say goodbye
to my dear rocket.
but as the rocket is now long gone
may we sing a new song
a song with some hope
a song, self moving
a proclamation that declares
our hearts no longer live in damnation
but in search of a deeper understanding.
a future is upcoming
and the future is always demanding
another rocket will shortly be landing
and the space station has room
for no freeloaders,

but on a moonshot exile
do not think about that guy or gal
but on what's above you now,
a sky filled with stars.
wherever you are
near or far
remember this,
the future is new every second
and those possibilities are endless.
it will be hard
but you'll find greener pasture
mountains that are higher
and maybe a partner
exists around the corner.
love harder
and more passionately
love with who you are
it's more freeing.

fusion pt.3 (musically wild)

crocodile rock

a wild crocodile sits on his rock
he was young
he and his friends have so much fun
but not for long.
the suited man with mighty hair
plots to take their air
relocate the heir.
this land
it has beautiful sand
a good place for a mansion.
it's also a good place for a crocodile rock
a place to harvest oxygen
and conserve nature
but suits are invasive
and pose true danger,
killers of the endangered
they do so with pleasure.
now my feet just can't keep still

nature deserves a better time
and yes
i'll make sure it will.
i step on the heads
of our lord's and governor's
if i must,
take me to the pilot
who will fly me to crocodile rock
where i will make my stand
where i will chant
"na, na na na na na. na na na na na."

misinterpreting 70's songs

ain't no mountain high

mountains are high
valleys are low
rivers are so wide baby.
i hear you wherever you are
no matter how far
call my name i'd be sure to hurry
make sure you'd never have to worry.
but maybe a few,
kilimanjaro knew
that love and dedication
decrease in value
in the face of desperation
and mount desperate
takes many souls,
souls that were happy
recklessly lovely
some lived in the valley
that was low enough.

so low in fact
they became trapped
and entrapment is so very different from entan-
glement
though both an inconvenience
one has a trail that leads to rivers
oh so wide.
so wide that horizon is shorter than the other side
such width humans can't surpass
and the life of these waters
poses even more complications
as you dodge bloodthirsty piranhas
barracuda
and the leech.
but distance always does damage
damage evolves from placing significant time
and space.
we are not lonely animals
we seek touch
even when we're not seeking,
or hiding
not even involving ourselves in the game.
we still desire

we are not in love with the cold,
but the coles that ignite fire.
listen baby
if you need me call me,
even though i know you won't
you say no matter where i am
you'll be there
but that was before i was here.
because there i was
and i needed you there too
though it was too much to ask.
i told you
you can always count on me
and for that i apologize,
i try to be
as honest as i can
but on that account
i was not speaking in truth
i spoke in wishes
that i couldn't follow through on.
there are mountains stronger and taller
valleys deeper and more meaningful
rivers that are faster and more dangerous
and for that i understand

and i do not hold it against

bad bad leroy brown

nobody told leroy to be the way he is
maybe he loves the way he lives
maybe he is the way he is
by the way we were raised as kids.
maybe he is the baddest
and that used to hurt,
but pain only lives as long
as tolerance is dead
and tolerance is always awakened
by persistence.
eventually the gut shots are absorbable
eventually you become dependent
to constant ailment,
but before that
rises desperation
and in that desperation
you find opportunity,
it's not always the opportunity
to break free of your attackers
just a chance to strike back
to not stand over
but simply stand up.

sometimes that means
wearing the face you hate
my bet says
he never wanted to be bad leroy brown
but great fear pushed him there
and our reaction
kept him locked in that cage,
so he kept wearing it.
it was the only path we left for him
how does someone move on
after being bad ?
you could be sad
but of the two
which is truly worse ?
sadness is anger
without the power,
defenseless and weak.
but badness delivers
greater dominance
and that's all we left for leroy,
so before you run and hide
or perhaps
as you do so
remember leroy was once a child

just like all of us.
and he's always going to be a human being
same as the rest of us he's seeking,
something

rocketman

lost in the never ending
always expanding
sea of stars,
far beyond the atmosphere
or the place i call home.
where i can't hear others' voices and opinions
where i have no expectations
each day i float
i count stars,
on my return mission
and it's going to be a long time.
i miss earth more than i thought i might,
skipping stones
watching birds in flight
blue waters
beaches in sight,
surfing always felt so right.
now i count the days
until i see her face
i'm a rocketman
burning up the fuse up here along.
i've seen mars

i'm unimpressed
particularly with the way
one must get dressed
there's not much beauty
it's really not soothing
i remember home
how everything used to be so groovy.
i forget how much longer now
but i think it's going to be a long long time
our planet is sacred
unmistakably the one of one,
i wish you could understand
that our place in the solar system
cannot be replicated.
our abuse of our soil
can no longer be tolerated
we can no longer be bullied by governments
who bank hope on the return of a rocketman
he's never coming back.
we place our faith in scientists
to rebuild on the moon,
our dream come true
trash that floats off to space
easier for you.

where there's no climate to change
our lives can rearrange,
who needs free space nowadays ?
we're torching our only home
to bonfire
some are nervous
others don't care,
but it's safe to assume
a lack of movement is still there.
allow me to remind you
the causality of standing by
while your feet catch fire.
those costly burns
and it'll be a long time
a permanent sort of time
before we touch down here
again

hey jude

hey jude
i need to know
was it so bad ?
did you go get her ?
did you remember to let her into your heart ?
did you find a way, to make it better ?
i certainly hope so
i definitely want to know
if you found a way to make it with her alone
given your fear,
fear of letting someone else in
after all you've been through
i just wonder,
if there's a way to make that better.
i know how it feels
to feel like you have to carry everyone and everything
to have everyone tell you it's unnecessary
while not picking up any of the weight,
and it makes you think a little colder.
hey jude
when you found her

how did it make you feel ?
did you speak right then
or did you freeze at first ?
did she make it into your heart,
did it make any of this any better,
why do you wait for someone to perform with ?
perhaps you know that
it'll always be just you
and you're waiting for someone to carry the world with
even if it's just for a minute.
hey jude
is carrying the weight alone all that bad ?
what if sad songs
only get sadder ?
suppose if you remember to forget about the past
then you can last
long enough to see it get better
better
better
better.

don't stop me now

don't stop me now
i'm on a roll
ready to risk it all.
seen things i wouldn't have dreamt of
been in places i've never wanted to go
but go i did,
and did, did i do
now what i've done.
i look back on
i question
i beg for second chances
i carry my regrets
though i watch how my peers carry themselves,
not so different from how i went about life before
and i wonder who's got the right picture
who's bearing the right armor for life's war ?
those who approach creatively logistical
finding flaws,
avoiding the too wild,
the alcohol.

or those who embraced a good chase with poi-
son
and it's taste
but to go through life
not looking back
not thinking about all you once had
running from repercussion and judgement.
refusing to make amends
instead
a full force charge ahead.
"don't stop me now
i'm having a good time"
though i do wonder
where they feel that pressure from ?
for i feel the only person who tells me to stop
in my expedition
for correct navigation
of the path to explanation
is me,
and my occasional faltering
gut that says
"let's just have a good time".
but greatness is giving up
good fun

greatness requires expedition to find
everything under the sun.
i've surrendered my soul contractually
to do what's wise
to think twice
and stray from ways
i've already taken.
all this
in pursuit to be something more,
my peers ask not to stop them
for the same fear
a runner would feel
if she stopped running the race,
something would catch up.
they fear their decisions and life patterns coming back
while catching their breath,
putting them on a side of the line
where they would have to rectify
what they've broken and destroyed,
deal with a heading that hurts first.
i am asking my peers
my friends
my family

not to stop me now.
my time is not good
i do not float
i have no reminiscence of lady godiva,
and though my gut tells me to
try the path again
i've walked it
and chose not to stay.
don't stop me now
as my paths take me far away
i was not made to tire
or follow familiar ways.
but i hope that when i've finished my course
i leave behind a trail that leads to treasures
maybe yet,
a list of alternatives
for my peers to turn to
when they give up on their race
against their fears
and responsibility.

outro

so what's to gain
from misinterpreting old songs
of fun and fame ?
like the crazy little thing called love
it's not something
i'm so sure of.
so instead i present a love letter
to the greatest decade to date:
dear old seventies how i admire your strange passion
from good good mornings to finding the right woman,
there was no shortage of the bizarre.
the man of rubber-bands
and the operator
who knows not how it feels,
to the summertimes
with half bred honky cats,
to escaping to the end of the line.
in the fall of philadelphia
where finally we met camellia
we put on the boogie shoes

and built buttercups until mr. blue
introduced me and you.
and i turned to stone
as you made my dreams come true
i was forever a member of the love train
bound to the chain
where we twisted the night away
and shook our groove things.
we found the best way to get through today,
is with a bit of kung fu fighting.

fusion pt.4 (musical beginnings)

what was written
over chords and rhythm
now hidden.
when you can't do anything right
pick up the pen
start to write.
and when people say everything you do
is wrong
it's time to sing a song.
not developed
nothing too long
now enter my collection
of one-hundred thoughts.

100 thoughts

1. some people are meant to be chased,
never caught.
but it's the pursuit
that brings us such immense joy in life

2. someone please
tell me how,
i can make it in this
town,
i'm so tired of falling
down,
just to get back up again.

3. never say no to something
that you'll never forget

4. in the eye of almost every believer
i see the fear,
that what they pray to someday see
will never appear.
whispers of a deceiver

5. a new years resolution
comes packaged as fact
in this version,
i don't have to determine
how to love myself
in order to spread love
to someone else.

6. a pure power
with this board
i cut through powder,
the mountain my slave
and i
the master.

7. cool air is installed into my bloodstream,
my lungs breathe best
in frigid conditions.
i carve my skate's edge
into this frozen layer of water
with a certain knowledge,
this is home.

8. so you begin your swim
not knowing exactly how far you can go,
you just know
you want to go further than anyone has gone
before.

9. i am not a member of familiarity
this makes me dangerous,
this makes others overly cautious
they study me like an animal,
they keep their distance
no zoo animal dare get closer
then the fence will allow.
if they did
they may just find the wilderness

10. driven by drawings and cartoons,
i take little seriously.
like drunken buffoons

11. you can't love me anymore
than you can love a box of memories.

12. our monsters never leave
they become our friends.

13. the worst feelings
aren't the ones that hurt the most
but the ones i can't process
or write about.

14. my life,
my love
it will always belong to the trees.
and my feet,
will forever rest upon
those dirty paths
that take me back
to the places that evade human impact.

15. i think i've had enough
i think i'm tired of
thinking about how we could of
of been enough.
i know we almost loved
almost had love
i almost had enough
for us.

16. there's hidden subplots
in most things that are said

17. sometimes it's good to let the charge burn out,
return to reality
experience the world we live in
once more.

18. in competitive competition
we forget that every loss
is lost if we don't learn,
and every win
is winless with those who can't practice
their path to victory.

19. imagine your lifeline being powered by electric current,
that's our generation

20. there's no visible finish,
my unfinished focal lengths
and my acute depth of field
make sure i'll never see anything
more than two steps in front of me,
but who needs to see
when you can be free

21. i'm chasing something greater
than green paper
i'm chasing something that might not make
sense
in this hour
or the one after,
but i trust that it will
later

22. good writing
it's like saying,
good depression

23. i need you
like a spoon needs a fork
but a knife keeps up apart

24. the fact that you still follow the life
of someone you hate
simply for a follow back,
is everything wrong with this generation

25. my dear rugged coastline
how i long to taste your refreshing air
dance on your rocks.
and gaze at the power of the ocean
you contain

26. people distracted by actions
actions disguised as passions
souls starving for healthy rations.

27. some will get to enjoy this world
the rest only focus on surviving
and you swear,
that we all get fair chances.

28. she came to understand over time
that i cared for her
that i was preparing land for her
and quickly she realized it wasn't land
that she wanted.
i came to understand
that it wasn't land she needed
it wasn't land she desired
she deserved mountains.
and now i'm left to wonder
what to do with the land.
once a gift
now a memory
do you give it away to whoever's next ?
or do you run away
and try to forget.
good land
now spoiled soil
we try our best to move on
love on
and try again.

29. why do i feel like
if i ran the streets naked
the rest of my life
less people would run and hide
more people would rejoice my name
and celebrate my fame.
this world was assembled backward
a true shame

30. funny
that the funniest people
feel the saddest thoughts

31. those hateful people
who we call rude and evil
i wonder if they feel
the same way i do.
not as much anger or bashfulness
not enough energy to carry on with this
gave away a lot of love
and got none back.
pain and torture starts to stack
it attacks where i stand
we all need to feel appreciated
or life becomes bland.
those who feel hateful
feel dead inside,
those who have love
but it's hard to find,
those who need help
finding where it resides,
yet all we do is spit and criticize.

32. don't worry
if you have to try,
don't worry
if you scared to fly,
don't worry
if the mountains too high,
because on this day you'll never die.
don't worry
if you get too scared,
don't worry
if it's all unfair,
don't worry
if you ascend into the sky,
because on this day you'll never die.

33. we are creatures who try too hard
to try and set new bars.
one day we'll be on mars
driving our fancy cars, the future looks scary
why worry about looking so crazy ?
just be yourself and be united
everyone else is uninvited
don't worry about a thing
except for dancing in your crazy dreams.

34. so i took that life away
i took it to watch it fade,
through it all in the hurricane.

35. we live and we do
but eventually we grew,
our hobbies outgrown
jobs were found
replaced what we loved
and told us
money is enough.

36. you call me cynical,
i give what i'm given.
doesn't sound that different from your religion

37. i am depressive
to those who approach aggressive
i am impressed
by those who admit they are a mess
i am old
for the stories i've told
and young
for the scars that stung.

38. i can smell it
it's in the air,
somethings you don't find
everywhere.
the rugged coastline
the deep blue sea
it calls my name
it's where i need to be.
dear old friend
who i
call the oceanside,
won't you come meet me
in the place where i reside.

39. i know this won't last but
neither will we.
try me

40. always think of what could be
never what is,
it's a part of me
to dream of what i've missed

41. the other side of the mountain
it's easy to get there
hard to conquer

42. the dish will never be better than the produce
producing good fruit
will always bear good existence.

43. when our eyes lock
i don't see the person,
i see the monster.

44. vulnerability breeds honesty
honesty can follow down two paths;
one that's free
the other catastrophe.
all outcomes come to reality
completely free,
you can have the vision to see
who you are
and who you want to be.

45. is it what the story tells
or is it
how the story is told ?

46. don't take the time
to explain to me the waves.
don't bother me with death
i'll find the grave.
i care little about tomorrow
i live for today.

47. my job, as a writer
is to push you
from the path of proper
to the path of progress.

48. all my love
is for the planet,
all my time
spent studying its grandeur,
and living in its wonder.

49. i often hear 'i have faith in my god to care for my planet'
but i never hear 'god has faith in us to take care of the planet'

50. i enter the room
same way i always do,
with my surfer attitude
and my hair dew.
i'll admit
i've never worn shoes
and i never intend to

51. some days i still feel the rays of your energy
i hope in those days
it means you're feeling better in that place.
there's more step in your life
and it's spilling into mine

52. the best views
are the ones of endless blues
listening to ocean tunes.

53. i love things that are more simple than people
maybe that's the true ripple,
to why i am nothing more than a social cripple

54. in the end,
it seems
to chase after just one thing
will always leave you disappointed

55. i hear whispers from the trees
i see the gloom in the weeds
i smell pollution and dirty streets
the bitter taste of poisoned mountain peaks
i feel sadness on my cheeks
for the call is left unanswered
for weeks.

56. hidden in history
hides great meaning

57. alone, is when i socialize
because in that silence
i have your company
once again.
when i'm alone
you cannot fade
and when i close my eyes
our adventures begin
like they never stopped.

58. i want nothing more
than for you to be happy
but i hope i never have to see it
with my own eyes,
because i can only pretend to be happy for you
while wearing a disguise.

59. it became old being the bearer of bad news
but bad news and bad views
are all that comes from my heart
that's been torn in two,
i wish i could see everything differently
but i am cursed with only seeing what's true.
today's been another sad day
all i can think about is you

60. what you call negativity
i call careful pessimism.
for i know
every stride towards optimism
is a step deeper into vulnerability
and those are chances
i'm not ready to take.

61. "it's shit like this that makes me not trust the world"
and who said this place should be trusted in the first place ?

62. some of us are dead inside,
trying to find something to keep us alive
a heartbeat,
life support,
something.
anything.

63. without writing
i wonder what differentiates me
from other species.

64. i'm falling for you
but i don't know a thing about you
why won't you let me go ?

65. you're different
but exactly the same
i've decided you're brilliant
but i know you're lame.
just another player in the game
maybe you are different
but you'd rather be tame.
what a shame

66. for my perpetual hatred
to the
oh so cold weather
i do question,
how i came to be
such an
oh so cold person.

67. that energy you see
deep inside of me
you think it's something happy,
is a passion of fury.
the monster seen
in the mirror of my dreams
it's just me
but angry.

68. it is true
that with great money
you have freedom to do
whatever you'd like,
but is it not also true
that if you do whatever you'd like
you will eventually have great money.

69. two roots
branch from the same tree
but i head west while you,
the east.
you head for the mountaintops
and i,
the sea.

70. belief is a fashion of concentrated energy within it comes binding both in sacrament and duty,
within that is the rewards of enlightenment; spatial understanding
all this gift wrapped with the purpose of addressing self worthiness.
what do i believe you might ask,
well, i believe in fire
i believe in water
i believe in the trees
i believe in such things
that will always do the right thing.
i believe in irregularities,
and if you see something that you consider crazy
then you've answered your question.

71. because in this generation
we spend our lives in rooms with closed doors
locked doors.
i lived life in the hallway
surrounded by the horrors
that scared everyone off
and i did it alone.
i climbed up stairs
going floor to floor,
until i found an empty room
and put my foot in the door.

72. there's few things more aggravating
than observing multiple layers of stupidity.
people who complain about overflowing trash
who have filled the compost bin with recyclable material.
people who call others stupid
when they themselves do not possess enough intelligence
to call out their own stupidity.
and of course,
anyone taking a selfie.
anywhere.

73. what's the difference between logical calculations
and creative decisions ?
one you're born with
the other comes later
and is written on paper.

74. how can i sleep with so many questions in my head
how can i sleep when i'm already dead,
you never sleep once your tombstone's been read.

75. you'll never be respected
if you give them what they want
show them what there's not.

76. gaze in wonder at the open blue sea
a coastline to see,
nowhere i'd rather be.
because here
i can be me

77. you're only good enough to rot
you impersonating
generational robot.

78. my stubbornness
determines this,
i will
get
where i want to
go.

79. try everything once
after that,
follow your gut

80. you guys have life in your eyes
you deserve the camera.
my eyes are true testament
to how i feel in life,
dead inside

81. i walk slow because i hate reaching my destination
adventure is the greatest invention.

82. it's 2020
we have science behind anything
we have research put into everything.
and still
our politicians fight over concrete
not an eye batted towards our environment
the news cares more for celebrities,
and degrading presidents to be,
i just want everyone to see
the planet needs you and me.

83. now that you've seen me for what i am
i don't feel the need to force the smile
i hope you don't dread
that you may never see it again.

84. there's always a moment of fuck..
but don't stay there
okay,
what to do.
plans of action
not resentment

85. to determine what is for certain
to pull back the curtain
to divulge in person
to unload the burden,
though my condition will only worsen
for this version
has immersion with introversion
and prefers bourbon
over conversation.

86. what's left of me,
i no longer know who he is.
he's a monster, i no longer wish to see
no me to return to, no
the old me
is finished.

87. reality is whatever we make it
if you can dream it
it just became real,
at least to you.
whether or not the world ever
discovers these mental wonders
is dependent on your capability
to show them.

88. i suppose i'm just as victim as all
our society spreads stories of torture and failure
the great fall
we forget about the occasional win
and it's grandeur.

89. in my journey
i forgot
the comical nature
of destiny,
that is
humanity

90. even when i can't find the words to say
even when the bad comes my way
my love for you stays the same,
today
tomorrow
and everyday

91. beauty is so easily contained in few words
but i must confess that it is the legal document
that will change the world.

92. i am a runner standing perfectly still
for unlike the other athletes
i see the track,
and refuse to move on other people's demands
i run my own path.
until i find my direction,
i stand my ground.

93. i am quiet
but my silence is rarely
the absence of opportunity,
and more an overabundance of patience
as i wait steadily,
for openings that lead to the doorways
of the soul.
and i steadily ignore
the words that originate in the mouth
for they lack sustenance.

94. i am not a full fledged inspiration
i am only the metalworks of genius
occasional passive pieces
of the great intelligence
we seek to possess.

95. the moon may not always carry the most beautiful face
but the moon will always be the moon
in every phase.

96. remember that the jokes we tell
are the only jokes that exist in the galaxy.

97. we're not where we should be most of the time
i spend far too long looking down
waiting to see if the sidewalk will shine.
when i should look high
if anything is going to shine
it's going to be in the sky.

98. intergalactic stories
of far away places
where you can mine love in quarries
and ride unicorns on ferries,
a strange place.
but vast and beautiful
this is where stardust grazes faces
welcome to the universe.

99. why did the doe cross the road ?
maybe because we put the road
in the doe's home.
we are human
we are selfish
and love to impose.

100. one hundred one hundred,
one hundred,
seems so long ago
i saw injustice in the world.
driven and absurd
began to manage word for word
what i found
to be profound,
to be for sure,
examined what could get worse.
one hundred
one hundred,
one hundred,
day by day the words i hunted
escaped like toxins
that leave me haunted.
prescribed by nonsense
i see such little progress,
since
ninety nine
ninety eight,
and ninety seven.
i fear we'll all be dead
by short poem one hundred and eleven.

fusion pt.5 (the short essay meets the new day)

in case we get away
here's another series coming your way,
about our favorite days
of the year
the holiday.

Holidays

from presents to graves
to gatherings around the table
on thanksgiving day.
we think of happy days
and firework displays
and the year long resolutions
from which we strayed.
for built on these days
a foundation was laid
and on it we built tradition.
we built song
and set in stone
that on these calendar marked events
we shall not go about our business casually
instead we will gather as one united family.
and on this day we invite those
who have nowhere else to stay,
to join us in party
in celebration.
and to embrace
a new face
to a new year.

October 31

goblins and ghouls
zombies with pools
of blood on the ground
bodies dropping make familiar sounds.
sounds profound but now
in the dead of night,
a growl
dread and fright
your breathing is tight.
you shield your eyes as
it comes into sight...
just a deer
oh dear,
inside you cheer
for it's not a killer
just a simple critter
looking for a pasture
to fill her.
dark clouds and big storms
lightning strikes start fires
to keep us warm
burning flesh attracts the swarm

you pray that the ghost
brings no harm.
this is the day of the dead
today starts the beginning of the end
tonight the stories get bent
tonight it ends,
with the witch's head.

November 28

the table is set
it's time now to eat.
everyone pulls up a seat
laughter and peace,
gather round for there's a feast
pumpkin pies by the plenty
so we all get a piece.
we eat till we can't anymore
the plates are filled until we say
'no more'
thanksgiving could not come a day sooner,
today we needed some family
we needed some release
we say thanks to tradition
we say thanks for the memory
we say thanks for our raising
and the tradition
never-changing.

December 25

gift giving and given gifts
present themselves around neatly placed or-
naments.
there's a tree and there's lights
there are long nights
free of fright,
terrors and haunts feel the warmth
of the glimmering candle
that sits on the mantle,
we so often forget
the light that sits there
is not for us exclusively.
light's greatest purpose
is to give meaning
to the dark
and to the lost.
we don't all receive candles on mantles,
some of us don't even have homes
it's a lost and broken world.
governments that fill stockings with coal
and we let them act so bold
let the holiday stand as a reminder

if not a call to action,
for every present taken should one not be given
?
for every meal had can you save a bite
for someone who hasn't eaten ?
a call to action
isn't that the true purpose
to the holiday season ?

January 1

branches dead
snow covered and back again,
they now give
new breath.
a year like a mountain
we climb
and we persist,
a year like a fountain
replenishes and ages,
everyone chases after the aura of newness.
lifestyles get old
jobs get old
our gadgets and gizmos
reach expiration dates,
like milk cartons
and the food that reaches our plates.
here before us is a chance
one we don't have to create
but is given
a freebie.
the opportunity to new discovery
as the final fireworks boom

and new calendars begin to bloom,
remember what it is
that keeps you true
and in the aura of what is now new
do what you have to
to become more you.

fusion pt.6 (calendars are shapes)

though not on page
and certainly off topic,
a calendar is a square shape.
and with it we have relationship
it often commands our days
tells us our relatives' changes in age,
allows us to plan ahead for our drinking ways
on friday's.
the calendar serves as a medium
a shape for the time
now begin to see how shapes
take over much of our lives,
and represent much.
to waste more time
on this fusion stands as crime
i now present
geometric.

Geometric

the line formula

graph paper can be crumpled and torn
but what's written
remains.
you can swear at it
call it names
but what's written
remains.
we may hate what's contained on our page
but until we bring an eraser,
our page will represent the relationships of our lives
in documented fashion.
we are all rays
starting in one place
and extending as far
as our page will let us.
we become intertwined into circles
and squares

lost to infinite loops
and inescapable edges,
these shapes shape our lives
and occupy space on our pages.
eventually after we escape from our shapes
we learn to reframe,
our shapes exaggerate and conjugate
taking us to new faces
in new places.
we find new shapes
and we incorporate the new imports
into important extortions.
until the page is full
we evolve,
eventually our shapes begin to revolve
around that which is most important to us,
perhaps another ray
or some larger shape.
your goals are hidden somewhere on your page
already
but there's still so much for you to explore,
they'll wait for you there
exactly where they are
and you'll meet them

right in their place.

circles

we all fear the permanent.
the career
long term loan
the afterlife
the marriage,
what's scarier than something
that has no end ?
the power in that is indestructible
no matter how many lines you put inside
how many you surround with
the circle cannot be broken.
its wheel,
forever spinning
the axis always perfect
so much to fear in that.
because once you have it
you can't go back
if given endless cash for a week
could you go back to life before ?
we all have circles
things we can't live without,
the things we feel we need.

it's why we chase closure
so we can look back on the past
and see as few of mistakes as possible
so we can look back
and watch all those wheels spin fluently.
we like what is sharp
pointy
jagged
it gives color
it delivers new shape.
a world of wheels wouldn't be all that interesting
we need the points to connect to one another
but we lie if we say
we don't chase perfection
we all want to be wheels
with a million wheels captured inside of that wheel
never letting a radii get too close to the inner arc.
and to that i might never understand,
i suppose the act is for appreciation
to stand on others
to be on the peak.

perhaps i have broken too many circles to follow
but i find love in points
i believe we all do,
maintain your circle
and when one of your smaller circles breaks
don't cover it.

angled

sharp changes of direction
a sudden change to a constant perception
believing what you thought was true
but it became misconception.
it doesn't have to be life changing
one-hundred and seventy nine degrees is still angle grazing,
sometimes it's the smallest change
that makes you the most amazing.
and these angles will give you your shape
through these angles
your world perceptions will drape like a superhero's cape
a staple of who you are,
a symbol of who you're going to be,
a queen of near and far,
the captain of the sea.
the person who you've always wanted to be
a sharp ninety degrees from the bachelor's degree
you're currently achieving.
the safe and steady

one hundred and eighty,
too fearful to be ready
they never get any
thing.
angles move forward
sometimes backward
they'll make you cry today
but you'll laugh a lot after.
even falling apart is better than stagnation
complacency is the greatest complication,
like a face half shaven
or an alien invasion
they all ask the same question.
what's your angle ?
what makes your shape ?
three-hundred and sixty degrees
to show what makes you great.

segmented

time is constant
it never bends,
time is important
to remind us our lines have ends.
every timeline recorded in history
every great memory for you and me
no line ever exceeded it's book,
it's bound by page.
some will live forever for the stories we tell
and for the outrage
they can dispell.
but every heart has a shelf life
until we learn to become eternal,
'till that age
we must find ways
to do things with days,
and combine days with
adventures and quests
missions and tests
skills, and all the rest.
we try and be the best
because what else is there ?

you know your line can only have so much page left
and the pen can run dry at any given moment,
that being a moment we never wish for.
the soul lost early
many don't believe
that it could happen to them
the thought of death has overwhelmed so many,
the thought of segmented life is indeed scary
not accomplishing all you can in this life instills anxiety.
to add a shot clock to that
can make the strongest people become stiff
and it should,
as you sit on the couch
and say the 'i coulds' and 'i woulds'
remember,
there's only so much ink in the pen
and the page is running thin.
you know what you have to do,
do what you feel needs to be done
do what you want to
before your page is done.

square

beauty is jagged
these four corners represent where perfection
reaches stagnation.
for who should stop
before becoming the circle ?
an unstoppable wheel you can hurdle,
the box is but the edged circle
building an image that may have started with
beauty,
yet somewhere along the way
dipped deeply into insecurity.
i'm certainly no square or circle
i'd be lucky to have an attractive angle,
but it hurts most dearly
to see the square.
you stop and stare
for you know they were once capable of so
much
but before perfection
they became caught in pretension
resulting in permanent suspension
of any hope for resurrection.

dear squares,
i wish you'd see your snares
you're so close to being the greatest of all of us
but instead you're stuck in the mud,
gathering dust and rust.
some may escape this place
but as the shape of a page may suggest
there is no way that is easy.
you must find humility
honesty
and true family,
find ways to say thanks
to those who have done you right.
with that you just might
find yourself back where you've started
on the journey to being
a full circle.

triangles

within us all
the entirety of the human race
and extended beyond to the universe
points to something.
no one word is acceptable as summary
no entity to prove itself correctly,
the only word i've found to establish closely
is beauty.
as deep as we've now gone,
to the far reaches of an ever expanding galaxy
the depths of trenches
and into the core beneath our own feet
there lies a question,
what is it that we seek ?
it would be naive to believe
we search to say we searched.
or to say we saw because we wanted to see,
why would someone fly
past the point of breathable air
and sail straight out of the atmosphere ?
what is the research of our ocean's deepest
depth going to change ?

none of us will ever go there
nobody will ever stay there for their lives
seemingly
there stands no real answer as to why we
should care.
but therein lies one head to the triangle,
beauty.
we are infatuated with our senses
and the expansions of our horizons,
we want to feel so small that we forget what we
are
perhaps in hopes that we become something
more.
it's why we sit around in meetings,
and dream of our beginnings
and do research on everything.
though beauty answers so much
it fails to answer everything,
the second head to the triangle is said to be
meaning.
as a human alone
isn't built of stone,
why do we deserve the privilege
to be this free ?

the king species
amongst everything
we know is living.
we have the power to close anything
from climbing to creating
from destroying to inventing.
the accomplishments and progress of humanity
is undoubtedly special,
but why have we been able to do as we've done ?
there was a time when humanity could not even sing a song
motivation is birthed by belief
and meaning
and consciousness.
look at the athletes
who say they won't stop getting better
until their play is close to holiness,
for every aspect of life
we see those who pushed humanity farther
than it's gone,
motivated by the chance of greater meaning
and enlightenment.
the last head of the triangle may just be

love,
love ties together the other two.
with love installed,
your sense of meaning and beauty
are upgraded beyond capacity.
suddenly you see the great importance
to mean something.
with beauty
you can feel love in a new way
for love isn't linear,
it comes in different shapes and sizes
it comes in great and small quantities
and it becomes our job to determine
how love will come out of us,
as it's love that will leave our imprint on this world.
nothing else.
as we operate within our triangle estates
we narrow down the universe
into a more simplistic being,
we travel farther
to find greater beauty.
and we find ourselves in new ways
to establish new meaning.

and we harness the magic of love
to find new feelings.
travel the triangle,
test yourself
and find limits.
and don't forget to triangulate focus
on what most of us
end up missing entirely
love.

tools

as you learn the importance of your paper and
it's existence
you must know too,
it is in fact
your paper.
though many will come along,
shapes will be drawn,
lines will exist
drawn by no one,
this will still be your page.
it still is within your power to control a great
deal,
even as it feels as uncontrollable as a car in the
air
the page will eventually fall back in your lap,
and when it does
you better have a plan.
for an unforeseen chain of events begins to
stand
and without control
it spreads like weeds,
it's scribbling things

and tearing seams
that hold your page together.
distress not,
for once you harness
the logistics of a compass,
the arc you seek becomes yours to draw.
to power the peace of a protractor
can be the factor
that decides great success and patience
or disaster.
and the fullness of a free handed pencil
with this comes your uniqueness
and the morals
to be good
or to be terrible,
the story is yours to write.
but not everyday will bring such truth
just as success today
isn't proven as such tomorrow,
catastrophe is life's loan
that it's borrowed.
though with the right tools
you'll see the way through the window that reflects

the light,
and the light that sits in waiting
at the end of the tunnel.

outro

now that the tools have been gathered
and the formula is understood
and in place,
it's time to put away the paper for a while.
live life with pace,
as many have come to see
if you look at the paper too often
you'll forget what you're called to be,
lines and shapes
angles and tools
used to change the world
to change others,
to become the circle
and to triangulate the precise place on the paper
that is best made to support this upcoming segment of life.
the formula is not meant to count the days remaining
or make day by day historical changes,
today is about reframing history
bending the page to your liking

erasing shapes and building tools.
tools to become a page
that's unlike the others,
to bring truth to the world's deepest lies.
in the end
most pages will be filed away
a global collection of ordinary people who had ordinary days,
but a few will be pinned and framed.
those who lived another way
those who so carefully crafted plans of great action
those who saw the rest
and determined to be best.
your days are still early
even after thirty,
do not be discouraged
do not begin to hurry
the time ahead may be blurry
but today you fix what's in front of you.
take a minute to determine the shapes around you
the lines not erased
and the space left on the page to run,

for that's truly just the catch
isn't it ?
to run on paper
leaving footprints unlike any to be seen before
footprints to bring others to the door
where we see many more
join the running course.

Fusion pt.7 (fusion of effusion)

literary effusion
the act of unrestrained,
heartfelt written action.
perhaps one of the deepest acts of passion
like a perfect circle
no cracks to stop this wheel.
this is a short series
of the crazy mind
of a crazy youth
and it's the truth,
ruth.

effusion in three parts

chapter one

trying to find answers
as to what i haven't fully destroyed.
i pick up pieces of broken glass
and as it cuts my hands,
i start to understand myself
a little bit more
a complete waste of time and thought.
don't tell me i'm 'unique'
i know what it truly means,
it means i'm confusing,
i lack common competence.
i am aware.
i didn't ask to be like this
given a chance,
i'd be someone else by tomorrow.
my mental state's internal destruction
is fate
i wasn't born to be thought of

in the world
but out of it,
dead or alive
it's my afterthought that survives,
not me.
like a firecracker we do not remember who set it into the sky
but we remember the fireworks left behind.
i'm not developing stories,
just one that says
i can't fucking overcome the smallest of things
and i can ruin the best of beings.
these things i need to keep me sane,
the people that keep my head in my brain,
i am less than worthless.
i'm a terrorist
terrorizing my own system.
tell me i'm a failure
degrade me in your heads
and let your words
do the rest.
but don't expect me to defend myself,
i have nothing to block with.
don't expect me to jab back at you,

i have no weapon to fight with.
this world is stupid,
the people are worse,
and i am the worst of them.
a walking curse

chapter two

rest my dear heart,
you're taking it too far,
this life isn't that serious
and it's made to fall apart.
rest my dear heart,
forget your mind and feelings,
give up on having any dignity
drink bottles until you can't breathe,
pick fights in the streets.
it's time for us to go back to
what we were always meant to do.
have fun
drop the regrets
fuck the stress and having respect.
rest my dear heart,
we're going back to the start,
before all the misery,
where those pretty girls were missing me
where we steal things that are free
we'll be a happy mystery.
fuck what the people say
we'll drink in their faces

throw up in places when we get wasted.
this life wasn't meant to be thought about
it was meant to be experienced.
so take the fucking cab
it's time to be delirious
there's no more time to be sad.
no more crying
no more feeling so bad
there's plenty of fish in the sea
ones bound to be as odd as me.
rest my dear heart,
we took it too far,
let's get wasted by the pier
whisper obscene things in people's ears.
saturday night's alright for fighting
that's what i wanted to hear.

chapter three

it's a good anthem
but it's not you.
that's good banter
but don't flatter.
you're scared to touch the cup again
i've never watched the wings flutter faster or farther
when there's conflict at the front door.
saturday is for resting,
because we've fought ourself all week
a seven day mental battle
that leaves the soul weak
the body meak.
as we peak around the corner expecting fight
we cower.
i don't deny
a fist fight is exactly what you're looking for
how accomplishing it'd be to finally win a battle,
but that's not victory.
we weren't fighting that person
our fight is a mad scramble for sanity
a scrambling squabble

trying to keep the eggs from getting scrambled.
i know you speak like the person you want to be,
but if it's not who you are
how long can you keep the act up ?
we've seen this routine before
it never lasts long.
stay true, stay steadfast, and hellbent
stay fucking alive for christ's sake.
and keep the eyes focused forward
you're either looking down the barrel
or you're looking for the next one.
Always.

Fusion Finality

'till now
the balance of order
amongst the chaos has been sound.
sections have placed themselves well
knowing their purpose shall be served,
their voices heard.
though now comes in finality
in the book,
as in life
this is when it becomes unbalanced
and crazy.
the sky now hazy as we see
five boats left in the sea,
with still plenty
left to offer
you and me.

a pile of rejects

a stance on what freedom could be

in my never-ending pursuit of freedom,
today i made a breakthrough.
freedom
as i know it
has no physical restraints,
no spot on a map,
no bounds,
and can encompass all things.
freedom cannot be explained in words,
much like faith
it is something that must be felt
or shown.
so through these examples,
perhaps you too will recognize freedom's face
as i am starting to.
the acts of freedom are done through action
and movement,
to ride board on top of wave

that is not the freedom.
the freedom comes from the acceptance
the peace you make within the knowledge
that every day at sea could be your last.
knowing that sharks are the prince's of the water
and wave danger rises as waves get taller,
with freedom comes accepting your fears.
the words are the source of refreshment
that can't be consumed in liquid form,
but is processed in the mind
and soul.
sunlight that kisses you with warmth,
dancing trees that sing with the rustling leaves,
all this beauty embodies what it means to be free.
to be set apart
in a place where you can go anywhere
at anytime,
and with it comes fears.
snakes and bears
weather changes
and strangers.
but once you accept those fears

and still
you go,
you move.
you are free
free to do anything
free to be expressive
the freedom to believe
you can be whoever you want to be.

dear me in the past

i'm afraid so much of what we hoped to become,
still lives only in the shadowlands
of an unforeseeable future.
i have failed you,
breaking the promise to never conform
i find myself still the enslaved,
still serving many of the same masters
teachers and directors
coaches and captains.
i walked into the trap
now left defenseless
i am rotting in this alien planets' elements.
no sign of home,
no feeling of freedom,
i can feel each breath i take
dying as it touches the air.
every pump of blood
a strain,
and a lasting feeling of pain.
i have entered a war zone
i have now seen what happens

when you become so lost in chaos
that you discover order.
for the reckless decisions of old
to build a machine
and travel the world
was chaotic
but not idiotic.
though as that ship came to port
i hesitated to board,
i was filled with concern,
for somehow so deeply rooted to chaos
order found its way back to my head,
and told me to consider my life
after death.
as i sat
and i thought
i found selfishness in my heart,
maybe the grandeur of adventure is
at best,
self centered.
the world around begins to burn
you'll soon see,
i found myself between many crossroads.
crossed roads

crossing across tossed thoughts
cross-eyed blinded by streetlights
and tongue-tied by it's glow
so bright.
i could no longer see the sky that night,
i blinked
to see the enemy caught me.
i lost everything and everyone
my one word of advice moving forward,
to trust no one.
the ones you love
are true to themselves and smart
but,
they don't see the possibilities,
they fail to believe in the wild
they still have an abundance of order.
now i'm lost in a prison
where chaos is a sickness
and i face treatments
until eradicated.
without your inner chaos
and wild heart
what will be left ?
an ordinary man

who lives a life the way everyone else can.
without freedom,
under the thumb of hands unreachable,
faces unseen,
dreams now deemed dead.
dear me in the past,
these breaths are getting heavier
and the heart's condition is dire,
with no break in the clouds
please remind me of the sound
a wave makes
as it breaks down.
and remind me again of the smile
that saved me for a while.

how chess is like everything in life

life is like chess
there's a lot of moving pieces,
there's an opponent who makes the board
a mess.
though the opponent plays behind
a darkened shadow,
he has many names
and he may be the opposite of hallow
or truly
exactly that.
though he bears many names
and wears many faces
the status of his existence is regarded as fact.
some of us believe behind the veil is indeed
a mirror
and that all along
we've been playing ourselves,
the good in us losing the game to the horror inside.
some of us believe in more
like a beast that attacks from offshore,
others hold faith in existential lore.

whatever the face
and whatever the name,
it holds true
our lives are expressed through chess games.
these pieces make up who we are
the way we play is promise to how we attack life
our over-aggression cost the life of the knight tonight.
and the addiction
nearly killed the queen.
bishops teach that not everything is up and down
but crosspaths
and sideways side paths
still send us in specific directions.
yet we all arrive with a similar question in the end,
to castle or not to castle?
with rook moving to protect king
your heart now solidified
you're prepared to venture,
to push the opponent to rethink
giving you time to become offensive.

start to win the life you lost back.
whatever he's taken off the board,
even if it's every pawn, bishop, and knight
even if he took the queen,
now is your chance to take back some
breath for your lungs.
synchronize your heart to the beat of a new drum
remember where you came from
and how far you've come,
check.
now on the offensive
it's time to see how far you can push life
into your bloodstream,
yet be careful not to lose what you have re-gained
it's not always wise to throw yourself
so far into a new situation,
that's a move of desperation.
desperation can either turn to inspiration
or devastation
and given your opponent
he'll do everything to push for disaster.
instead plan your moves.

instead you do as life does,
you let life make its move
and then you check it.
and you continue to check it.
until the opportunity arises
life opens its door,
and you make sure you capitalize.
remove the vail
and see the terror of a helpless opponent.
with the tears of victory
you can finally say,
checkmate
to the long game.

dear bubba (goodbye best friend)

i know that i'm heading onto something
for the better.
but as i hold onto you
this very night
your trust placed so faithfully,
so intensely,
i can feel it radiating out of your little body
and into my soul.
i have to wonder why i'm choosing the things
that i am.
how could i ever leave this behind ?
how could i ever leave you behind ?
you are my best friend
my most faithful friend
my stubborn protector
who's studiously watched over me
as i grew into the man
i am now.
and i watched as you grew into yourself
your personality so unique,
your humor so playful
your habits so clean

you are an example that should be followed
and i have learned so much from you.
i want nothing less than to be by your side
every minute of every day
studying your incredibly scheduled days.
some will only know you as dog
but i will always know you
as the only one who always understood how i was feeling
and how to make me feel better.
and how i can walk away from that
in pursuit of something so medial as education
it's beyond me.
it's staggering.
and frankly it's fucking stupid.
but something tells me
that if you one day sprouted two hands
stood on your back legs,
spoke a language
i could understand,
you'd tell me that i have to go.
that i have to go find something,
make something,
follow my brain

if i can't take my heart.
like when you are playing ball
but have birds to chase,
of course you want to keep playing
but the right thing to do
is scare away the intruders.
owning my mental land is so important,
there's a lot you can build there.
banks of important memories,
important information
like the closest park we can go visit,
i will miss you so very dearly.
i know it'll be a bit confusing for a while,
our bed is now yours to protect
until i return,
i know i leave it in the best hands..
or paws.
never forget that no matter where i am
i wish you were within eye shot,
and you will never escape my thoughts
for even just a minute.
i love you pup.
though i don't think that even expresses it
deeply enough.

a book of poetry

this book.
it stands as my documentation,
my own personal history
my ups and
mostly my downs.
sometimes cheerfully aggressive
others unfortunately depressive.
tough seasons and years come naturally,
sometimes lasting longer
than it takes for me to write a book.
and i know i am in part to blame,
i could hold harder
to a more positive outlook,
i should try again
to find something joyous.
but in this past year,
this time spent
i dealt with a great many defeats.
i was given more blows
than the average punching bag
and it shows in the writing.
i'd be lying to say it doesn't bring me guilt,

i wish to be a voice of encouragement
and a guide to positive happiness.
but in reality,
i study the faults
i observe the flaws
and they bother me
too much to live in peace.
yet
but perhaps in great time
the clouds overhead will clear,
and light will touch my bridle skin
once again.
so with all the truly broken feelings,
i'm reminded that it's a product of living more wilder than others.
galaxies and geometry know that
change is constant and constantly moving closer
on the page to my existence.

Fusion's End

much can happen once fusion ends,
but one fact remains
fusion is energy.
and raw energy leaves much room
for many things.
how you may take the energy
synthesized from these pages
is entirely in your power,
today in this hour
may you think of it as a chapter
closed.
the last of petal
of the last rose.
you have climbed a mountain.
for even reading
a short book as this
in our generation,
is deserving of celebration.
i'm grateful that this journey
was one that could be shared.
take care.
-r.w.

there's no telling
what's held in the time
that's after this day.
for that
there will never be a way.
and there is no safety
in what happens
when our bodies lay,
but
there is today
and
today
is a good day